Happy Valentine's Day!

To:

_____

From:

_____

Date:

_____

To my Valentine

Happy Valentine's Day!

Expressions of Love for the One I Cherish

Honor Books
Tulsa, Oklahoma

Happy Valentine's Day!
Expressions of Love for the One I Cherish
ISBN 1-56292-756-6
Copyright © 2000 by Honor Books
P.O. Box 55388
Tulsa, Oklahoma 74155

Introduction

Love knows no boundaries. It is the essence of existence and what makes our lives worth living. While love is timeless, the celebration of Valentine's Day comes but once a year. It's that special day when we go beyond the everyday expression of our affection to show the ones we love how much we care about them.

So make this Valentine's Day a beautiful memory you will treasure forever. Cuddle up now and read this beautiful little book to your sweetheart. . . . How do I love thee? Let me count the ways.

We are all born for love.
It is the principle
of existence.

—Anonymous

Did you know?

The first U.S.-made valentines were crafted by a college student, Miss Esther Howland. Her father, a stationer in Worcester, Massachusetts, imported valentines every year from England. Esther, however, decided to create her own valentine messages and began importing lace, fine papers, and other supplies. She employed several assistants, and her brothers helped market her valentines. As one of the first successful career women, her sales amounted to about a hundred thousand dollars annually—not bad for the 1830s.

Romantic Suggestions

 Put chocolate kisses in his dresser drawer.

 Bake him a heart cake.

 Send him a balloon bouquet or flowers with a special note.

Love looks not with the eyes, but with the mind; and therefore is winged Cupid painted blind.

—William Shakespeare

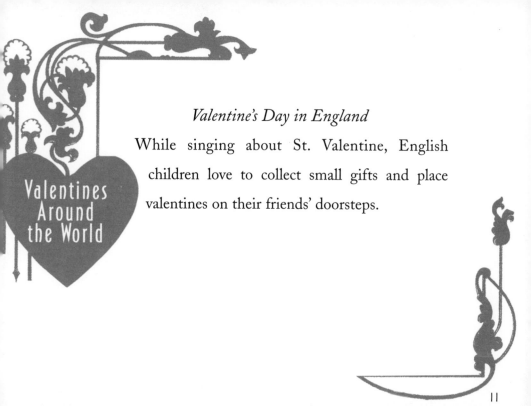

Valentines Around the World

Valentine's Day in England

While singing about St. Valentine, English children love to collect small gifts and place valentines on their friends' doorsteps.

Life is the flower of which love is the honey.

–Victor Hugo

Did you know?

It was once thought that birds chose their mates for the year on February 14th. Doves and pigeons mate for life, and therefore were used as symbols of fidelity.

What the world needs now, is love, sweet love. I feel it when I sorrow most: It is better to have loved and lost than never to have loved at all.

—Alfred,
Lord Tennyson

14

Love sought is good, but given unsought is better.

—William Shakespeare

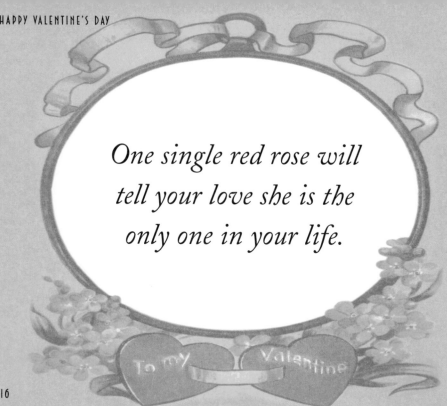

*One single red rose will
tell your love she is the
only one in your life.*

To my Valentine

Each color of rose has its own meaning:
Red and white together mean unity.
Pink stands for grace and gentility.
Yellow symbolizes joy.
Orange or coral roses suggest desire.
Burgundy compliments your sweetheart's
unconscious beauty,
and white roses say, "You're heavenly!"

Love is two souls with a single thought, along with two hearts that beat as one.

—Anonymous

Romance in a Jar

Fill a jar with romance coupons for a candlelight dinner, an evening of dancing, a picnic for two, a night at the movies, or watching the sunset together. Have your valentine close his or her eyes and pick a "love activity" from the jar each week.

Love comes from God and those who are loving and kind show that they are the children of God.

—*1 John 4:7 TLB*

Cupid's Love Tea

Ingredients

1 cup water

¼ cup honey

1 cup apple juice

¼ teaspoon cinnamon

6 cranberry flavored
tea bags

Bring water and juice to a boil. Stir in honey and cinnamon. Add the tea bags. Remove from heat.

Let stand for one hour. Add 6 cups of cold water. Pour into glasses with ice. Sit back, sip, and fall in love.

*If you have love in your heart,
you always have
something to give.*

—Anonymous

Love Coupons

Make a love coupon that you print yourself and leave on your spouse's pillow. Here are a few suggestions:

 Breakfast in bed

 Dinner for two

 An evening stroll

 One big bear hug

Did you know?

A young Frenchman, Charles, Duke of Orleans, was one of the earliest creators of valentines, called "poetical or amorous addresses." From his confinement in the Tower of London after the Battle of Agincourt in 1415, he sent several rhymed love letters or "valentines" to his wife in France.

If you would be loved, love and be lovable.

—Anonymous

A Romantic Fantasy

My sweetheart and I are walking hand in hand along a secluded white beach with a beautiful aquamarine ocean beside us. A soft breeze rustles our hair. We stop and kiss.

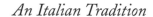

Valentines Around the World

An Italian Tradition

On Valentine's Day in Italy, it was customary for a young woman to awaken before sunrise and look out her window for the first man she could see. He would either be the man she would marry or he would look like her true love.

Helpful Hints for Husbands

Take half a day off of work and prepare a lovely candlelight dinner for the two of you. Surprise her with soft, meaningful music, a bouquet of flowers, and two tickets to see her favorite romantic film. The next morning, serve her breakfast in bed.

. . . Or book a small hotel for a weekend break in the country and don't tell her until you get there. Make sure the room is stocked with fresh flowers, candy, and scented candles.

♥

Valentines Around the World

A Danish Tradition

In Denmark, it was customary for a man to send a woman a valentine *gaekkebrev,* or joking letter, that contained a rhyme and was signed with a series of dots to represent his name. If the woman guessed his identity correctly and notified him on Valentine's Day, he would reward her with an Easter egg on the next Easter.

*My love was warm; for that I crossed
the mountains and the sea,
nor counted that endeavour lost
that gave my love to me.
If that indeed were love at all,
as still, my love, I trow,
by what dear name am I to call
the bond that holds me now.*

—Robert Louis Stevenson

"Shall I Compare Thee to a Summer's Day?"

Shall I compare thee to a summer's day?
Thou art more lovely and more temperate:
Rough winds do shake the darling buds of May,
And summer's lease hath all too short a date:
Sometime too hot the eye of heaven shines,
And often is his gold complexion dimmed;
And every fair from fair sometime declines,

By chance, or nature's changing course untrimmed;
But thy eternal summer shall not fade,
Nor lose possession of that fair thou owest,
Nor shall death brag thou wanderest in his shade,
When in eternal lines to time thou growest;
So long as men can breathe, or eyes can see,
So long lives this, and this gives life to thee.

—William Shakespeare

Did you know?

The tradition of becoming engaged on Valentine's Day is
not new. As early as the 17th and 18th centuries, a suitor
would give his lady love a ring set with some type of
precious stone to pledge his intention to
marry her. Today, diamonds are
the stone of choice.

The most wonderful of all things in life, I believe, is the discovery of another human being with whom one's relationship has a glowing depth, beauty, and joy as the years increase. This inner progressiveness of love between two human beings is a most marvelous thing; it cannot be found by looking for it or by passionately wishing for it. It is a sort of Divine accident.

—Sir Hugh Walpole

A Beautiful Love Story

Elizabeth endured hell on earth during her formative years. She was one of eleven children born to a father who was an oppressive, dictatorial tyrant. His angry rages often sent sensitive Elizabeth to her bed with any variety of ills.

It wasn't until she was forty years old that Elizabeth met Robert. He did not see her as a middle-aged invalid. Rather, he saw her as a beautiful, talented woman just waiting to blossom. Robert loved her with all his heart and withstood several brutal confrontations with Elizabeth's controlling father before he finally won her hand in marriage.

Glowing with love for each other, the couple traveled the European continent, marveling at God's wonders and at their own love. At forty-three, Elizabeth gave birth to a healthy baby. Their lives were full and beautiful. In great joy, Elizabeth wrote to her husband the incomparable words of "How Do I Love Thee?"—perhaps the best known of her Sonnets from the Portuguese. True love embraced Elizabeth Barrett's life when she became Elizabeth Barrett Browning.

"How Do I Love Thee?"

How do I love thee? Let me count the ways.
I love thee to the depth and breadth and height
My soul can reach, when feeling out of sight
For the ends of Being and Ideal Grace.
I love thee to the level of every day's
Most quiet need, by sun and candlelight.
I love thee freely, as men strive for Right:

I love thee purely, as they turn from Praise:
I love thee with the passion put to use
In my old griefs, and with my childhood's faith;
I love thee with a love I seemed to lose
With my lost saints—I love thee with the breath,
Smiles, tears, of all my life!—and, if God choose,
I shall but love thee better after death.

—Elizabeth Barrett Browning
from Sonnets from the Portuguese

Love is patient, love is kind. It does not envy, it does not boast, it is not proud. It is not rude, it is not self-seeking, it is not easily angered, it keeps no record of wrongs. Love does not delight in evil but rejoices with the truth. It always protects, always trusts, always hopes, always perseveres. Love never fails.

—1 CORINTHIANS 13:4–8

A Love Letter

This unconditional love I have for you captures the very essence of what a valentine is—a heart so committed to give you the best of who I am. Like flowers in the fields, the beauty of the forests, and the vastness of the ocean, my love for you can only bring joy to my soul. I love you with all my heart, now and forever.

—Anonymous

Did you know?

According to *Good Housekeeping* magazine, 70 percent of men buy flowers for their spouses on Valentine's Day, but only 13 percent of women buy flowers for their husbands. Six percent of men buy flowers for their mothers, compared to 21 percent of women. Four percent of men and 7 percent of women buy flowers for their daughters. Only 8 percent of men buy flowers for their friends, in comparison to 14 percent of women. And the most popular Valentine's Day flower? The red rose.

Having trouble deciding on a gift?

Here's what women *really* want for Valentine's Day:

 Flowers

 Jewelry

 Tickets to an event

 Perfume

 Candy

Chocolate Fudge Sauce

Ingredients

³/₄ cup heavy cream

2 oz. unsweetened chocolate

2 oz. semisweet chocolate

2 oz. milk chocolate

2 Tbsp. brown sugar

2 Tbsp. butter

In a small heavy saucepan, heat cream just to boiling. Take it off the heat and whisk in unsweetened, semisweet, and milk chocolate, chopped, and brown sugar and butter to melt. Swirl over vanilla ice cream.

Fun Things to Do with Your Sweetheart

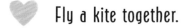 Fly a kite together.

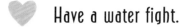 Have a water fight.

Climb a tree together.

Go roller-skating.

Make snow angels.

 Play miniature golf.

 Take a bike ride.

 Play Ping-Pong.

 Go window shopping.

How do single women celebrate Valentine's Day?

 Giving cards

 Calling friends

 Preparing special meals

 Going out to dinner

 Giving flowers

 Throwing parties

The only real security is not in owning or possessing, not in demanding or expecting, not in hoping, even. Security in a relationship lies neither in looking back to what it was, nor forward to what it might be, but living in the present and accepting it as it is now.

—Anne Morrow
Lindbergh

Chocolate Truffles

Ingredients

8 oz. semisweet
chocolate chips

²/₃ cup heavy cream

2 Tbsp. butter

1 pkg. chocolate kisses

unsweetened cocoa
powder

In a small heavy saucepan over low heat, melt semisweet chocolate chips and cream. Take the pan off the heat, and beat in butter. Freeze until firm. Roll 2 tablespoons mixture around a chocolate kiss; toss in unsweetened cocoa powder to coat. Chill before indulging. Makes 12 to 14 truffles.

I lie beside you and sometimes it seems
That every day is just living a dream.
We've grown together through passing years.
We've shared our secrets and our fears.
We've seen the sun rise. We've seen the sun fall.
I know that you know I gave you my all.
I've held you when you've laughed.
You've held me when I've cried.
So I promise to always stay in love
With that magical light
in your eyes.

—Anonymous

Perfect Chocolate Frosting

Ingredients

1 stick (¹/₂ cup) butter or margarine

²/₃ cup cocoa

3 cups powdered sugar

¹/₃ cup milk

1 teaspoon vanilla extract

Melt butter. Stir in cocoa. Alternately add powdered sugar and milk, beating on medium speed to spreading consistency. Add more milk, if needed. Add vanilla. Frost your favorite cake.

$\mathcal{Love}$ is happiness, love is aggravation, love is sadness, love is motivation. Love is comforting, love is endless, love is mesmerizing, love is selfless. Love is devotion, love is commitment, love is about emotion, love is heaven-sent.

—Anonymous

What particular group of people receive the most Valentines?

Teachers.
Next come mothers,
wives, and
girlfriends.

What Is Love?

To love very much is to love inadequately; we love—that is all. Love cannot be modified without being nullified. Love is a short word but it contains everything. Love means the body, the soul, the life, the entire being. We feel love as we feel the warmth of our blood, we breathe love as we breathe the air, we hold it in ourselves as we hold our thoughts. Nothing more exists for us. Love is not a word; it is a wordless state indicated by four letters.

—Guy de Maupassant

More Romantic Suggestions

 Hold the chair for your sweetheart when she's seated for dinner.

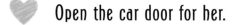 Open the car door for her.

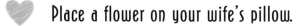 Place a flower on your wife's pillow.

 Write a love note and slip it into a book she's reading.

 Take a quiet walk together holding hands.

Write your sweetheart's name in the snow.

Make time for a pillow fight.

Write a special message on the bathroom mirror using lipstick, soap, or shaving cream.

 Buy an antique key and give it to your loved one inside a valentine; tell your sweetheart it's the key to your heart.

 Take a hot-air balloon ride together.

 Snuggle up and take turns reading a book out loud together.

Words that men love to hear:

I believe in you.
I want you.
I feel safe with you.

Words that women love to hear:

I cherish you.
I need you.
I adore you.

To my Valentine

When the Heart Is Full of Love

There is beauty in the forest
When the trees are green and fair.
There is beauty in the meadows
When wildflowers scent the air.
There is beauty in the sunlight
And the soft blue beams above.
Oh, the world is full of beauty
When the heart is full of love.

—Anonymous

A wise lover values not so much the gift of the lover as the love of the giver.

—Thomas à Kempis

Did you know?

There was a time when girls and boys wrote their own
Valentine sentiments on homemade cards.
Even with smears of white paste and a misspelled word
or two, these were some of the more popular verses:

I wish thee health;
I wish thee wealth;
I wish thee gold a store;
I wish thee Heaven
after death—
What could I wish
thee more?

Roses were made to blossom;
Cheeks were made to blush;
Arms were made to rest in;
Lips were made to . . . Oh, hush!

Cupid took aim—
Zing went the dart.
Every day is a valentine
With you in my heart!

*LOVE gives itself;
it is not bought.*

–Henry Wadsworth Longfellow

Let all that you do be done in love.

—*1 Corinthians 16:14 RSV*

Why do I love you?

Perhaps it is the smile you wear upon your face;
or the way you know the perfect time, the perfect place.
Though it could be the gentleness of your heart.
Or the way you make me feel, as though
we will never part.
Just maybe, it is in the soft words your lips speak.
For with simple words you make my knees draw weak.
It may be the twinkle I catch from your eyes.
Or the rainbow I see, now appearing in the sky.

Is it that you sneak into my thoughts every moment of the day?
Or could it be the warmth I feel when no words are needed to say?
Perhaps it is simply unexplainable magic, You and I.
Of course it is a miracle; one which we cannot deny.
The truth of the matter is, I have found completeness in you.
There is nothing too small nor too large;
nothing that I would not do.
It may be the little things that you always give to me.
No matter the rhyme or reason, with you is where I wish to be.

—Anonymous

Gravitation cannot be held responsible for two people falling in love.

—Albert Einstein

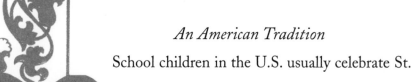

Valentines Around the World

An American Tradition

School children in the U.S. usually celebrate St. Valentine's Day with a party at school. Prior to the party, the children make a decorated box with a slot in the top. During the party, the children distribute valentines to their classmates' Valentine boxes. Mothers bake decorated sugar cookies for the kids, and the rest of the afternoon is spent opening valentines.

Love Is Forever

On the day after Jack Benny's death in December 1974, a single long-stemmed red rose was delivered to Mary Livingstone Benny, his wife of forty-eight years. When the blossoms continued to arrive, day after day, Mary called the florist to find out who sent them. "Quite a while before Jack passed away," the florist told her, "he stopped in to send a bouquet.

As he was leaving, he suddenly turned back and said, 'If anything should happen to me, I want you to send Mary a single rose every day.' There was complete silence on Mary's end of the line, then weeping, she said, "Goodbye."

Subsequently, Mary learned that Jack had actually included a provision for the flowers in his will, one perfect red rose daily for the rest of her life.

*Remember . . . love is the link
that holds two hearts together.*

—Anonymous

So many marriages are rooted in passion. But to grow in depth, a marriage must not only be a "love affair," but a deep and growing friendship—a meeting not only of bodies, but of minds, hearts, and souls.

How special it is when a spouse says, "I married my best friend." Even more special is the spouse who says after many years of marriage, "I am married to my best friend!"

Did you know?

Despite putting his couriers in danger, Napoleon often
sent love letters to his beloved Josephine,
even while he was at the battlefront.

LOVE ever gives,
Forgives, outlives,
And ever stands
With open hands.
And while it lives,
It gives.
For this is love's prerogative—
O give, and give, and give.

—John Oxenham

Somewhere beyond the depth of your eyes
and the brilliance of your smile,
beyond the comfort of your touch,
beyond all these miles
there is you.

Fountains springing from the pools of my heart
you are their tide; you are the unventured sea.

Reading Frost on the beach at sunrise,
all the emotions stirred by those words
are you.

Even if all becomes nothing,
there will always be you
and the memories you've given me.
This thing my heart will prove
I can never forget you.

—William H. McMurry III

Love Just Happened

I don't know how it happened,
I just know that it's true.
Before I knew what hit me,
I fell in love with you.
We started out just writing,
then chatting every day.
Poured out our thoughts and feelings,
till our love showed us the way,
and this love I can assure you
is forever and a day.

—Anonymous

Serenade your sweetheart with popular love songs.

♥ "My Heart Will Go On"

♥ "I Honestly Love You"

♥ "Always on My Mind"

♥ "Just The Way You Are"

♥ "I Just Called To Say I Love You"

♥ "The Way You Do the Things You Do"

♥ "How Sweet It Is"

♥ "I Will Always Love You"

♥ "Stand by Me"

♥ "Wind Beneath My Wings"

How to Romance a Woman

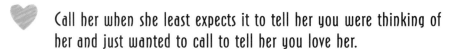 Call her when she least expects it to tell her you were thinking of her and just wanted to call to tell her you love her.

Leave sticky notes around your house where she will find them. On each note leave a brief message of your love.

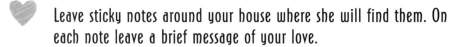 Hold her hand in public. Once in a while lean over and whisper in her ear that you love her and give her a kiss.

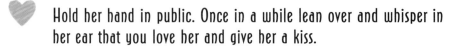 Give her a music box with a romantic song and tell her that it's to remind her of how much you love her each time she opens the box.

Send her flowers for no reason but to say you love her.

And now these three remain: faith, hope, and love. But the greatest of these is love.

—1 CORINTHIANS 13:13

Ideas for a Romantic Date with Your Spouse

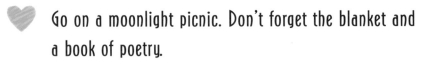 Go on a moonlight picnic. Don't forget the blanket and a book of poetry.

Sleep out under the stars, just the two of you.

Take a walk together under the light of a full moon.

Go dancing together.

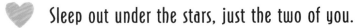 Kidnap your spouse for a prearranged overnight excursion to a local bed and breakfast.

Make arrangements to go horseback riding.

Who *so loves believes the impossible.*

—Elizabeth Barrett Browning

Sitting here and wanting
Not just anyone,
Desiring your every affection,
Needing no riches but instead
Candles and kisses
at a rainbow dusk.

—William H. McMurry III

LOVE is a great beautifier.

—Louisa May Alcott

My Sundae Valentine

Ingredients

2 scoops vanilla ice cream

1 large banana

1/2 cup of bottled chocolate sauce

red sprinkles

2 cherries

1 pretty glass dish

2 long-handled spoons

Slice the bananas into discs, and place in the bottom of a banana-split serving dish. Arrange the ice cream on top, and pour over the chocolate sauce. Decorate with red sprinkles and the cherries. Share with your sweetheart!

A Love Letter

I love you. Three little words that mean so much, yet seem to say so little. The way I feel about you, I need other words—bigger words—words that don't get used so often. I need a word for the heart-bursting joy that sets my head spinning whenever I think of you. I need another for the warm ocean of contentment I feel lapping around me when I think of you and the years we'll share in the future. And another for the determination I feel when I think of you—determination to make you so happy you will be mine forever. And the words for the desire you raise in me. But the only words I have are "I love you." I love you.

—Anonymous

Love comforteth like sunshine after rain.

—William Shakespeare

Love Is Eternal

Inside the wedding band that Abraham Lincoln gave Mary Todd was engraved the words, "Love is eternal." As Lincoln lay dying in a rooming house across the street from Ford's Theatre, where he had been the victim of an assassin's bullet, Mary Todd Lincoln twisted the gold band on her left hand. Had any other marriage ever undergone the strain of theirs? The war . . . the loss of a son . . . Mary's irrational behavior . . . and now this.

When the President breathed his last, someone in the room declared, "He belongs to the ages." Mary's response was, "He belongs to me. Our love is eternal."

Did you know?

At one time, people thought all emotions, whether fear, love, hate, or happiness, were all housed in the heart. Later, they believed the only emotion of the heart was love. That's why the heart symbol is still the symbol of love and Valentine's Day.

How do you say, "I love you"?

- Cantonese (Chinese) . . . .Moi oiy neya, or Ngo oi ney
- Czech . . . . .Miluji te
- Danish . . . . .Jeg elsker dig
- French . . . . .Je t'aime
- Italian . . . . .Ti amo
- Sioux . . . . .Techihhila
- Zulu . . . . .Ngiyakuthanda!

For what is love itself, for the one we love best? —an enfolding of immeasurable cares which yet are better than any joys outside our love.

—George Eliot

LOVE is like a tennis match;
you'll never
win consistently until you
learn to serve well.

–Dan P. Herod

To what shall I compare her, that is as fair as she?
For she is fairer—fairer than the sea.
What shall be likened to her, the sainted of my youth?
For she is truer—truer than the truth.
As the stars are from the sleeper, her heart is hid from me;
For she is deeper—deeper than the sea.
Yet in my dreams I view her flush rosy
with new truth—dreams!
Ah, may these prove truer than the truth.

—Robert Louis Stevenson

I've dreamed of this a thousand times before.
But in my dreams I couldn't love you more.
I will give you my heart until the end of time.
You're all I need, my love, my Valentine.
And even if the sun refused to shine,
Even if romance ran out of rhyme,
You would still have my heart
until the end of time.
Because all I need is you, my Valentine.
You're all I need, my love, my Valentine.

—Jim Brickman

A Day of Roses

Fill your spouse's day with roses. Place them on the pillow, in the shower, on the kitchen table, in the car, or any other place your sweetheart goes during the course of the day.

To my Valentine

Gift Ideas

Give your loved one a gift that will symbolize your love for each other now and in the future. Start a plant in a special place that will grow with your love. Or, get a gift you can share such as matching jewelry, complementary clothing, or membership to a club or organization.

To my Valentine

A Sweetheart's Book

Make a scrapbook that highlights your lives together. Use photos, ticket stubs, personal items, and other items symbolic of special events, places, and times you spent together. Wrap it in beautiful paper with lots of ribbon, and make it your special gift on Valentine's Day.

To my Valentine

How do I win your love; find the pathway to your heart,
the treasure that lies within?
Shall I be a thief in the night; sneaking past your guard,
to pluck it from your grasp?
Should I be a conqueror; sweeping it away before me,
locking it in a clasp?
Or maybe I should be a hunter, luring it into my trap,
until its fate is sealed.
Perhaps if I could be, then your heart, to me, you would yield.
Yet these things I will not be. I'm only a man. I'm only me.
I will not be a thief, and steal what is not mine.
I will not be a conqueror, for your heart I will not bind.
Nor will I be a hunter. I will not entrap what should be free.
I can only hope you will choose to share that heart with me.

—Paul Barton

Gift Hunt

Make gift-giving on Valentine's Day fun and exciting. Hide your gifts and leave romantic clues for your loved one to find and solve.

Love opens the most impossible gates.
Love is the gate to all the secrets
of the universe.

—Anonymous

Valentine's Day on a Budget

If you can't afford to buy flowers and go out to dinner, you can still make your Valentine's evening romantic. Prepare a romantic dinner together, dress up, and dine by candlelight. Then listen to soft romantic music while you feed each other dessert.

If you have love in your heart, you always have something to give.

—Anonymous

Valentines for Friends and Family

Fill a Valentine's Day coffee mug with cinnamon coffee and place it on that special coworker's desk. Finish off the gesture by perching a valentine on the telephone or desk chair.

Exchange "penny" valentines with coworkers and friends just like the ones your children exchange with schoolmates.

Hang a small, heart-shaped wreath on your neighbor's or friend's door with a valentine that says, "Thanks for being a friend." Take your baby to visit Grandma in a T-shirt that says "Totally Lovable." Or hide a special valentine for her in your child's diaper bag. Send pictures of yourself and your family in heart-shaped frames to the special people you love.

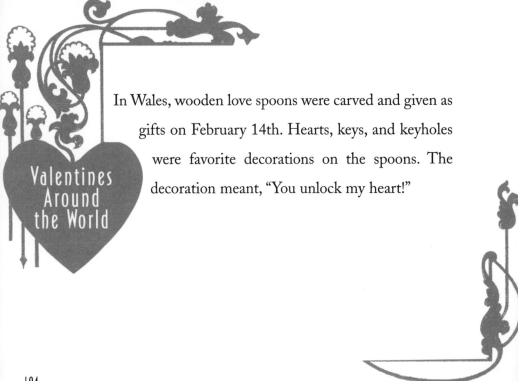

Valentines Around the World

In Wales, wooden love spoons were carved and given as gifts on February 14th. Hearts, keys, and keyholes were favorite decorations on the spoons. The decoration meant, "You unlock my heart!"

Grow old along with me!
The best is yet to be,
The last of life, for which the first was made:
Our times are in His hand
Who saith, "A whole I planned,
Youth shows but half; trust God:
see all,
Nor be afraid!"

–Robert Browning

Love cannot be forced;
Love cannot be coaxed and teased.
It comes out of Heaven,
Unasked and unsought.

—Pearl S. Buck

There are three things that are too amazing for me, four that I do not understand: the way of an eagle in the sky, the way of a snake on a rock, the way of a ship on the high seas, and the way of a man with a maiden.

—*Proverbs 30:18–19*

A Faithful Love

In A Time for Remembering, Ruth Bell Graham writes that when she was a teenager, leaving her childhood home in China for schooling in Korea, she fully intended to be an old maid missionary to Tibet. She did, however, give some thought to the particulars she would require in a man if she could ever be persuaded to marry. She wrote in her diary: "If I marry: He must be so tall that when he is on his knees, as one has said, he reaches all the way to heaven. His shoulders must be broad enough to bear the burden of a family. His lips must be strong enough to smile, firm enough to say no, and tender enough to kiss. Love must be so deep that it takes its stand in Christ and so wide that it takes the whole lost world in. He must be active enough to save souls. He must be big enough to be gentle and great enough to be thoughtful. His arms must be strong enough to carry a little child."

Did Ruth Bell find such a man in Billy Graham? Perhaps not on the day she met him as much as on the day they celebrated their fiftieth wedding anniversary.

She Walks in Beauty

She walks in beauty, like the night
Of cloudless climes and starry skies;
And all that's best of dark and bright
Meet in her aspect and her eyes:
Thus mellow'd to that tender light
Which heaven to gaudy day denies.
One shade the more, one ray the less,
Had half impair'd the nameless grace
Which waves in every raven tress,

Or softly lightens o'er her face;
Where thoughts serenely sweet express
How pure, how dear their dwelling-place.
And on that cheek, and o'er that brow,
So soft, so calm, yet eloquent,
The smiles that win, the tints that glow,
But tell of days in goodness spent,
A mind at peace with all below,
A heart whose love is innocent.

—Lord Byron

Surprise Your Children on Valentine's Day

Hide valentines and candy throughout the house and have a valentine scavenger hunt to find them. Tuck a valentine inside your child's backpack or inside the pages of a book you know your child will be using that day.

For those away at college, create a love survival kit and mail it off the week before Valentine's Day. Include goodies like chocolates and candies and a card letting them know how much they are loved and missed.

Give your child a big valentine teddy bear, no matter how old your child is.

Gifts that don't cost a cent!

 The gift of listening

 The gift of affection

 The gift of laughter

The gift of a written note

 The gift of a compliment

 The gift of a favor

 The gift of solitude

 The gift of a cheerful disposition

We can do no great things; only small things with great love.

—Mother Teresa

Write a Love Letter

When the honeymoon is over, most couples never seem to get around to saying those things that matter the most. So in addition to buying a Valentine's card this year, write your spouse a love letter on beautiful stationery, dab it with perfume or cologne, and tuck it in a purse or coat pocket. Your sincere sentiments will be the sweetest gift of all and cherished for years to come.

Romance Tips for Your Spouse

Women . . .

Call him "handsome," "rugged," and "strong," not "cute." Watch sports with him, even if it isn't your thing. Forgive him when he messes up. Spend time with him—no TV, no phone, no computer, just you and him. Tell him that you feel safe when you're with him. Ask him about his day and be interested in what he tells you. Encourage him in whatever he does. Take him to do something he enjoys. Always respect him—it is one of the things men treasure in relationships. Accept him for who he is.

To my Valentine

Men . . .

Listen to her problems. Let her rest her head in your lap.
Ask her for a dance when the two of you are alone together.
Play with her hair, women love that. Root for her sports'
teams, even if they're mortal enemies of yours. Make an effort
to get to know her family. Steal kisses while walking together.
Tell her she's beautiful . . . a lot. Remember all the dates she
thinks are important (the day you met, anniversaries,
and her birthday). Always be a gentleman . . .
hold the door for her.

To my Valentine

LOVE is friendship caught on fire.

—Anonymous

Incredible Fudge

Ingredients

2 pounds semisweet
chocolate, chopped

1 pint ice cream,*
slightly-thawed

1 cup pecans, chopped

Line an 8" or 9" square pan with foil and lightly butter the foil. Place chopped chocolate in medium-size glass mixing bowl. Microwave on full power for 1 minute and 45 seconds. Stir. Add thawed ice cream and beat until smooth. Stir in nuts. Turn into prepared pan. Refrigerate until firm; cut into squares.

*Use butter pecan, black walnut, mint, Dutch chocolate, anything but vanilla.

A Romantic Idea

Gather together a bunch of pictures of you and your loved one. Then find a song that means a lot to both of you. Have a videographer make a video slide show with your pictures and add the music to the background. You can really show him or her how much you care and have video memories to last a lifetime.

The more I think about it,
the more I realize
there is nothing more artistic
than to love others.

–Vincent van Gogh

*The perfect Valentine's gift is a kiss
and three little words:
"I love you."*

For Valentine's Day, my husband bought me flowers. There were five red roses, and in the middle was a white rose with red tips that "stood out." The card read, "Thanks for standing out in my life." It brought me to tears. It was the most creative and romantic thing anyone has ever done for me.

—Anonymous

Don't think that love, to be true, has to be extraordinary.
What is necessary is to continue to love. How does a lamp burn,
if it is not by the continuous feeding of little drops of oil?
When there is no oil, there is no light and the bridegroom will say:
"I do not know you."
Dear friends, what are our drops of oil in our lamps?
They are the small things from everyday life: the joy,
the generosity, the little good things, the humility and the patience.
A simple thought for someone else.
Our way to be silent, to listen, to forgive, to speak and to act . . .
are the real drops of oil
that make our lamps burn vividly our whole life.
Don't look for Jesus far away, He is not there.
He is in you, take care of your lamp and you will see Him."

—Mother Teresa

Never forget that the most
powerful force on earth
is love.

—Nelson Rockefeller

Ingredients for a romantic evening at home

 Scented candles

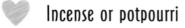 Incense or potpourri

 Romantic music

 Favorite beverage and glasses

Finger foods

Romantic movie

$\mathcal{T}o$ love is not to look at one another,
but to look together in the
same direction.

—Anonymous

$\mathcal{M}ay$ the love you share be
as timeless as the tides
and as deep as the sea.

—Anonymous

Love never ends.

1 CORINTHIANS 13:8 RSV

When the heart is flooded with love there is no room in it for fear, doubt, or hesitation. It is this lack of fear that makes for the dance. When each partner loves so completely that he has forgotten to ask himself whether or not he is loved in return; when he only knows he loves and is moving to its music—then, and then only, are two people able to dance perfectly in tune to the same rhythm.

—Anne Morrow Lindberg

Heaven *will not be heaven*
to me if I do not meet
my wife there.

—President Andrew Jackson

Short on Time?

Flowers, candies, stuffed animals, lingerie or boxers—these are all great gifts for Valentine's Day and can be found in most discount stores. Many of these items can also be found in any pharmacy or grocery store.

We hope this has proved a helpful
start but what shows your love
best of all is a precious gift
from the heart.

—Anonymous

Red Hearts

Ingredients

1 cup shortening

2 cups white sugar

2 eggs

1 tsp. vanilla extract

1 cup buttermilk

2 tsp. baking soda

4½ cups all-purpose flour

red food coloring

These make a pretty plate of Valentine cookies if you use different sized cutters and tint the dough in a variety of pink to red shades. Makes 3 - 4 dozen.

Mix ingredients in the order given. Divide dough and add enough red food coloring for desired shades of pink or red. Refrigerate dough for 40 to 60 minutes. Roll and cut out with heart cookie cutters. Sprinkle with sugar. Bake at 350° F for 11 minutes. Do not overbake.

LOVE is that condition in which the happiness of another person is essential to your own.

–Robert A. Heinlein

Ideas for a Romantic Date

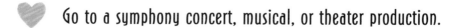 Go to a symphony concert, musical, or theater production.

Dance on a dinner cruise.

Ride in a hot-air balloon.

Spend the day at a theme park or zoo.

Go horseback riding.

Ride through the park in a horse-drawn carriage.

We *loved with a love that was more than love.*

—Edgar Allen Poe

An Old-Fashioned Date

Remember when you used to share a malt or shake with your sweetheart? Bring back those fun times by blending together two scoops of strawberry ice cream, a cup of milk, and some frozen strawberries. Pour in a tall glass and top with canned whipped cream and a cherry. Stick in two straws, cuddle up on the sofa, and share your frosty shake. Enjoy!

Life is a journey, and love is what makes that journey worthwhile.

–Anonymous

For where your treasure is, there your heart will be also.

—*MATTHEW 6:21*

Ideas for a Romantic Evening at Home

 Watch the sunset together.

 Picnic on your fire escape, patio, or backyard.

 Spread a blanket on the living room floor and have an indoor picnic.

 Read old cards and letters from each other to each other.

 Enjoy pizza by candlelight.

 Stay up all night eating popcorn and watching old movies.

Love doesn't make the world go 'round. Love makes the ride worthwhile.

—Franklin P. Jones

Love Letter Cookies

Ingredients

1 pkg. sugar cookie
  dough

candy hearts

Buy a roll of already prepared sugar-cookie dough. Instead of cutting it into round slices, roll it out on a floured surface and cut into rectangles. Fold up each side toward the middle, overlapping one edge to resemble an envelope, then seal with a small candy heart. Bake according to directions on the package.

A loving heart is the truest wisdom.

—Charles Dickens

Romance in a New Millennium

In past centuries, valentines have been delivered by servants, horse and buggy, airmail, and overnight delivery. But in this new millennium, you can send a love note over the Internet. There are several card services that will allow you to select an image, a poem, and a sentiment, or allow you to write your own, then send your valentine electronically. Use your favorite search engine to find one that's perfect for your sweetheart.

Valentine's Day is a celebration
of a perfect union of hearts.

-Anonymous

I already love in you your beauty, but I am only beginning to love in you that which is eternal and ever precious—your heart, your soul. Beauty one could get to know and fall in love with in one hour and cease to love it as speedily; but the soul one must learn to know. Believe me, nothing on earth is given without labour, even love, the most beautiful and natural of feelings.

—Count Lev Tolstoy
to his fiancee
(1856)

Did you know?

Ribbons, lace, and other frills are traditional valentine card decorations, but why? During the Middle Ages, a knight would ride into battle dressed in full armor, sporting a scarf or ribbon given to him by his lady fair. In fact, lace comes from a Latin word, meaning to ensnare.

The conclusion is always the same: love is the most powerful and still the most unknown energy of the world.

—Pierre Teilhard de Chardin

Love is an irresistible desire to be irresistibly desired.

–Robert Frost

Two Hearts as One Cookies

Ingredients

1 pkg. sugar cookie
  dough

strawberry jam

Roll out store-bought sugar cookie dough or use your favorite sugar cookie recipe. Cut out dough with heart-shaped cookie cutters and bake. When cookies are cooled, sandwich them together with strawberry jam for a sweet dessert to finish off a Valentine's Day dinner.

Many *things in life will catch your eye, but only a few will catch your heart.*

—Anonymous

A Kiss a Day

A West German magazine has reported the results of a study conducted by a life insurance company. The researchers discovered that husbands who kiss their wives every morning:

- live an average of five years longer,
- are involved in fewer automobile accidents,
- are ill 50 percent less, as noted by sick days, and
- earn 20 to 30 percent more money.

Other researchers have found that kissing and hugging releases endorphins, giving mind and body a sense of genuine well-being that is translated into better health.

A kiss a day may just keep the doctor away!

$\mathcal{LOVE}$ *is a beautiful dream.*

—William Sharpe

A Blessing for My Love

Beloved, I wish above all things that thou mayest prosper and be in health, even as thy soul prospereth.

—3 JOHN 2 KJV

So, fall asleep love, loved by me. . . .
for I know love, I am loved
by thee.

–Robert Browning

Movie Date

For a special date night at home, rent the 1950 version of Father of the Bride, starring Elizabeth Taylor as the beautiful daughter of Spencer Tracy. It's charming, funny, and sure to bring a tear of joy to your sweetheart's eye.

Did you know?

President Grover Cleveland was the first and only President to wed during his term of office. His bride, Frances Folsom, at twenty-one, is also our youngest First Lady ever.

Love cannot remain by itself—it has no meaning. Love has to be put into action and that action is service. Whatever form we are, able or disabled, rich or poor, it is not how much we do, but how much love we put in the doing; a lifelong sharing of love with others.

—Mother Teresa

Additional copies of this book and other titles in this series
are available from your local bookstore.

Merry Christmas
Happy Mother's Day

If you have enjoyed this book, or if it has
impacted your life, we would like to hear from you.

Please contact us at:
Honor Books
Department E
P.O. Box 55388
Tulsa, Oklahoma 74155
Or by e-mail at info@honorbooks.com